My First Acrostic

Poems From The East Midlands

Edited by Angela Fairbrace

First published in Great Britain in 2009 by:

Young Writers
Remus House
Coltsfoot Drive
Peterborough
PE2 9JX
Telephone: 01733 890066
Website: www.youngwriters.co.uk

All Rights Reserved
© Copyright Contributors 2009
SB ISBN 978-1-84924-478-7

Foreword

The 'My First Acrostic' collection was developed by Young Writers specifically for Key Stage 1 children. The poetic form is simple, fun and gives the young poet a guideline to shape their ideas, yet at the same time leaves room for their imagination and creativity to begin to blossom.

Due to the young age of the entrants we have enjoyed rewarding their effort by including as many of the poems as possible. Our hope is that seeing their work in print will encourage the children to grow and develop their writing skills to become our poets of tomorrow.

Young Writers has been publishing children's poetry for over 19 years. Our aim is to nurture creativity in our children and young adults, to give them an interest in poetry and an outlet to express themselves. This latest collection will act as a milestone for the young poets and one that will be enjoyable to revisit again and again.

Contents

Brant Broughton CE & Methodist Primary School, Brant Broughton
Jake Lawson (7)	1
Lucy Finch (7)	2
Philippa Coles (6)	3
Daisy Hardwick-Shaw (6)	4
Haydn Tear (6)	5
Hannah Balfe (6)	6
Joshua White (6)	7
Bayley Dunford (5)	8
Eloise Tate (6)	9

Canon Peter Hall CE Primary School, Immingham
Emily Clark (5)	10
Connor Armstrong (5)	11
Dawson Phillips-Burns (6)	12
Chloe Dibernardo (7)	13
Tia Dable (7)	14
Matthew Farnsworth (7)	15
Aaron Isherwood (7)	16
Jaylea Pulford (7)	17
Neil O'Toole (6)	18
Summer Melton (7)	19

Longmoor Primary School, Long Eaton
Isaac Brooks (6)	20
Jacob Watson (7)	21
Tommy Johnson (7)	22
Elliott Gilbert (7)	23
Chelsea Hubble (7)	24
Owen Sanderson (6)	25
Jay Littlefair (7)	26
Imarni Fearon (7)	27
Tyrese Lloyd Lindsay (6)	28
Jakihya Boyce (7)	29
Jack Cook (6)	30

Mapplewells Primary School, Sutton in Ashfield
Abigail Cranfield (5)	31
Aaleigha Brown (5)	32

Mornington Primary School, Nuthall
Yazlin Sheikh (7)	33
Freya Bird (7)	34
Jacob Morning (7)	35
Hana Ahmed	36
Lauren Thorpe (6)	37
Natasha Khosla (7)	38
Charlotte Hindson (7)	39
Ethan Wright (7)	40
Aimee Canavan	41
Charlotte Kirk (7)	42
Libby Dolman-Milner (6)	43
Nathan Robinson (7)	44
James Kirk (7)	45
Harry Franklin	46
Shiv Vasi (7)	47
Joshua Harris-Owen	48
Ellie Parkes (7)	49
Mya Sandhu-McKenna (6)	50
Bradley Francis (6)	51
Caashim Kotze	52
Ryan Wigg (7)	53
Nadia Zeidan (6)	54
Sophie Westbury (6)	55
Shivani Handa (7)	56
Hannah Davies (7)	57
Ishaan Jumbu (7)	58
Paridhi Pande (7)	59

Oakham CE Primary School, Oakham
Owen Burrill (7)	60
Philippa Stevenson (6)	61
Leah Crawford (6)	62
Louis Hibbitt (6)	63
Lucie McKie (7)	64
Teigan Palmer (7)	65
Chloe Hannah (6)	66
Angus Diggle (7)	67
Joshua Robertson (6)	68
Igor Lesney	69
Alice Aylward	70
Jessica Falconer (6)	71
Jack Cooper (6)	72

Georgia McNeill (6) 73

St John the Baptist CE Primary School, Spalding
Isaac Rudd (4).............................. 74
Lewis Haythorn (5)........................ 75
Ryan Gadd (5) 76
Daniel Plant (6) 77
Toby Keen (5) 78
Caitlin Seymour (5) 79
Ellie Blackbourn (6) 80
Oliver Keen (7).............................. 81
Max Bland (7) 82
Lia Carter (7)................................. 83
Harvey Wirkowski (5) 84
Hope Meadows (7) 85
Caitlin Langford (6) 86
Jamie Bertolaso (7) 87
Harry Harman (6).......................... 88
Ellie Whitcombe (7) 89
Charlie Wensak (7)........................ 90
Ocea-Lily Jarvis (5) 91
Erin Neve Freeston (4).................. 92

Sneinton CE Primary School, Sneinton
Novaya Bedward (7) 93
Jack Nuqul (7) 94
Shakira Daniel (7).......................... 95
Amelia Strangwick (7).................... 96
T'arnrie Simpson (6)...................... 97
Stevie-Lei Kinniburgh (7)................ 98
Shahaab Ahmed (7) 99
Chantelle Allwood (6) 100
Kate Armitage (6) 101
Amaan Aslam (6) 102
Joshua Colledge (6).................... 103
Jocelyn Do (6) 104
Joshua Musson-Screen (5).......... 105
Fola Okanlawon (5) 106
Gareth Pearce (5) 107
Caeden Perkins (5) 108
Emma Sargent (6) 109

Stanhope Primary School, Gedling
Lauryn Hewitt (5) 110
Coral Frost (5) 111
Emily-Jayne Sturt (7) 112

Holly Lamont (6) 113
Tamzin Forrester (7)..................... 114
Benita Rodman (6) 115
Amy Mosby (6) 116
Alex Sturt (5) 117
Flynn Perkins (6).......................... 118
Nia Everitt (7) 119
Georgia Wardle (7)...................... 120
Joseph Willey (7).......................... 121

Sycamore Primary School, Nottingham
Kye Wilson (5) 122
Sabian Mehmetaj (5) 123
Chloe Wilson (6) 124
Dylan Powdrill (6)......................... 125
Billy McGinty (6) 126
Jacob Jansons (6)........................ 127
Lashea Francis (7) 128
Mikhia Walters (7)........................ 129

Walter Halls Primary School, Mapperley
Christian Healy (7) 130
Imogen Hamlin (6) 131
Aisha Jobe (7) 132
Tamyra Sawyers (6)..................... 133
Caitlin McCullough (7).................. 134
Jasmine Bird (7)........................... 135
Wendy Ncube (7) 136
Maizie Simm-Grant (7) 137
Ashley Edwards (7)...................... 138
Elizabeth Fisher (7) 139
Andrew Jamson (6) 140
Amy Cunliffe 141
Ryan Bates (6) 142
Poppy Bawden (7) 143
Shourya Bhandari (6) 144
Henry Tien (7).............................. 145
Selicia Hickling (7)........................ 146
Makaay Ross (7) 147
Ethan Newstead (7)..................... 148
Jeneba Kanneh-Mason (6) 149
Oliver Thomas-Roche (7) 150
Kaliyah Sanghera (5) 151
Rio Foster (5)............................... 152
Thomas Justice (6) 153

Marian Eleshinnia (6) 154
Mia Harvey (5) 155
Kaira McGregor 156
Adina Brown (5) 157
Shannon Campbell (6) 158
Adrian Chamberlain (6) 159
Caleb Bird (5) 160
Hayden Barrows-Gayle (5) 161

Willow Farm Primary School, Gedling
Ellis Davenport & Jack Owen (6) 162
Carter Pateman & Rosie Walker (6). 163
Mckensie Withers, Lilly Hamed,
James Martin, Izabelle Hamblin
& Matthew Brookes (6) 164
William Barclay 165
Bob Banks (7) 166
Elyse Tizzard (7) 167
Josh Jackson 168
Freddie Talbot (7) 169
Laila Ahmed (7) 170
Holly Wild 171
Ava Hemsley (7) 172
Frazer Deabill 173
Taryn Pike (6) 174
Xander Beck (7) 175
Caity Cooke (7) 176
Michael Shepherd 177
Scarlett Leigh 178
Sonny Chapman (4) 179
Millieann Willis & Benjamin Shaw (5) 180
Murray Wild, Charlton Rooke,
William Redfern, Lucy Middleton
& Billy Jones 181
Oliver Holmes, Casey Griffiths,
William Galloway & Alyssa
Everington-Dale 182
Eve Blissett, Leon Blakey, Florence
Banks, Hannah Bacon
& Niamh Bailey (5) 183
Grabrielle Fowler
& Max Humber (6) 184
Zoe Hyland-Freshney (6) 185
Connor Macvickas
& Joseph Warren (6) 186

Maiya Needley
& Drew Chapman (6) 187
Harvey Widdowson
& Malachi Gregg (6) 188
Harry Bates & Emily Gomersall (6) ... 189
Millie Godward & Ben Morris (6) 190
Tom Oldershaw & Casey Lydon (6). 191

The Poems

My First Acrostic - Poems From The East Midlands

Jake

J ake is fun
A bike that's white
K yle is my brother
E xciting two brothers.

Jake Lawson (7)
Brant Broughton CE & Methodist Primary School, Brant Broughton

Lucy

L ucy loves dogs and puppies

U nder the covers I love to snuggle

C uddle sister and love Jemma

Y ounger sister Jemma, cute and cuddly.

Lucy Finch (7)
Brant Broughton CE & Methodist Primary School, Brant Broughton

My First Acrostic - Poems From The East Midlands

Philippa

P hilippa likes dogs, cats, bunnies and horses
H aving fun at school
I sobel is my sister
L ibby is a good friend
I like playing with Lucy a lot
P hilippa plays with her friends
P hilippa's been to the woods
A nd she played.

Philippa Coles (6)
Brant Broughton CE & Methodist Primary School, Brant Broughton

Daisy

D aisy likes dogs
A pples I like
I love my mum
S ometimes I ride my bike
Y is for yucky parsnips.

Daisy Hardwick-Shaw (6)
Brant Broughton CE & Methodist Primary School, Brant Broughton

My First Acrostic - Poems From The East Midlands

Haydn

H aydn is good
A t my house I play games
Y ou're good
D on't be sad
N ame is Haydn.

Haydn Tear (6)
Brant Broughton CE & Methodist Primary School, Brant Broughton

Hannah

H annah likes dogs
A cat comes to our house
N ew adventure
N ew adventure
A brother called Thomas
H annah *likes Eloise.*

Hannah Balfe (6)
Brant Broughton CE & Methodist Primary School, Brant Broughton

My First Acrostic - Poems From The East Midlands

Joshua

J oshua likes dogs
O n a horse is fun
S kating is fun
H orses are so, so fun
U nder the covers is snuggly and fun
A brother is fun.

Joshua White (6)
Brant Broughton CE & Methodist Primary School, Brant Broughton

Bayley

- B ayley
- A boy
- Y ellow car
- L ots of fun
- E xciting
- Y our dog.

Bayley Dunford (5)
Brant Broughton CE & Methodist Primary School, Brant Broughton

My First Acrostic - Poems From The East Midlands

Eloise

E loise likes rabbits
L ibby is my friend
O n a Saturday I go bike riding
I like Hannah
S ometimes I fight with Alex
E loise likes dogs.

Eloise Tate (6)
Brant Broughton CE & Methodist Primary School, Brant Broughton

Holiday

H ot holiday
O ranges
L ike strawberry
I ce cream
D ays are sunny
A nd
Y ellow sand on the beach.

Emily Clark (5)
Canon Peter Hall CE Primary School, Immingham

My First Acrostic - Poems From The East Midlands

Holiday

H ot holidays
O ranges
L aying down in the sun
I ce cream van
D aisy chain
A nd
Y ellow sun.

Connor Armstrong (5)
Canon Peter Hall CE Primary School, Immingham

Holiday

H ot holidays are fun
O ranges are juicy
L ollies are cold
I ce is wet
D onkeys are fun
A pples are crunchy
Y ellow shorts are good.

Dawson Phillips-Burns (6)
Canon Peter Hall CE Primary School, Immingham

My First Acrostic - Poems From The East Midlands

Unicorn

U se their magic all the time
N ever be nasty to people
I maginary creatures
C an't swing on trees like monkeys
O nly 100 years old
R eally big creatures unicorns can be sometimes
N ever kill a unicorn, it's not very nice.

Chloe Dibernardo (7)
Canon Peter Hall CE Primary School, Immingham

Kittens

K ittens are cute and cuddly
I love kittens lots
T wo years old
T hey like to play with string
E at cat food
N ot a bad pet
S o colourful.

Tia Dable (7)
Canon Peter Hall CE Primary School, Immingham

Zebra

Z ebras like to run
E at green grass
B lack and white
R un on the plains
A nd they run up to 40 miles an hour.

Matthew Farnsworth (7)
Canon Peter Hall CE Primary School, Immingham

T-Rex

T -rex eat other dinosaurs

-

R abbits hate T-rex

E lephants hate T-rex

X -rays show their bones.

Aaron Isherwood (7)
Canon Peter Hall CE Primary School, Immingham

My First Acrostic - Poems From The East Midlands

Monkey

Monkeys eat bananas
Only live in trees
Not a good animal for a pet
Kicks the tree for coconuts to fall
Every day the monkey is cheeky
You're a little bit like them.

Jaylea Pulford (7)
Canon Peter Hall CE Primary School, Immingham

Dragon

D ragons have sharp teeth

R eally are strong

A re good at fighting

G reat face

O ver confident

N ever eat me.

Neil O'Toole (6)
Canon Peter Hall CE Primary School, Immingham

My First Acrostic - Poems From The East Midlands

Kitten

K ittens like milk
I like kittens, they are cute
T wo years old the kitten is
T iny kittens like to play with wool
E very day they have fish
N ever tease them.

Summer Melton (7)
Canon Peter Hall CE Primary School, Immingham

Hot, Hot, Hot!

S eashores and seashells
U sually people get the pool out
M um gives us cold drinks
M um gives us biscuits
E very day I play in the pool
R abbits come out of their holes.

Isaac Brooks (6)
Longmoor Primary School, Long Eaton

My First Acrostic - Poems From The East Midlands

Falling Autumn Leaves

A firework might go off
U sually you see a bonfire
T he children get dressed up for Hallowe'en
U p in the trees you might see an owl
M um wraps us up warm
N ow it is getting colder.

Jacob Watson (7)
Longmoor Primary School, Long Eaton

Winter

W e have lots of snow
I t's cold
N ight-time it snows
T he snow is magical
E njoy the presents at Christmas
R abbits stay in their holes.

Tommy Johnson (7)
Longmoor Primary School, Long Eaton

My First Acrostic - Poems From The East Midlands

Autumn!

A lmost winter
U mbrellas keep us dry
T he leaves are red and gold
U sually it is cold
M um wraps us up warm
N o sunshine!

Elliott Gilbert (7)
Longmoor Primary School, Long Eaton

Snowball Fight

When I go out to play
It is cold
Now I am in the house
Teatime, Mum calls
Err some snow on the floor
Roll a snowman's head!

Chelsea Hubble (7)
Longmoor Primary School, Long Eaton

My First Acrostic - Poems From The East Midlands

Spring

S tay outside, it is sunny
P eer at a rose
R un in the grass
I watch the squirrels come out
N ice, sunny flowers
G rowing in the ground.

Owen Sanderson (6)
Longmoor Primary School, Long Eaton

Winter

W indy and cold
I can ice skate on ice
N ext day I build a snowman
T en snowballs rolled down the hill
E very day I take pictures of the snow
R eally cold.

Jay Littlefair (7)
Longmoor Primary School, Long Eaton

My First Acrostic - Poems From The East Midlands

Spring

S un is out
P ink flowers are coming
R abbits bounce around
I t is a bit cold
N ow baby animals are born
G irls and boys go outside.

Imarni Fearon (7)
Longmoor Primary School, Long Eaton

Summer Is Great

S un comes out
U p trees are leaves
M um gets us ice cream
M any children play outside
E veryone loves summer
R ooms are tidy.

Tyrese Lloyd Lindsay (6)
Longmoor Primary School, Long Eaton

My First Acrostic - Poems From The East Midlands

All About Winter

W inter is the day thunder comes
I t gets windy at night
N ow we get lightning sometimes
T rees get leaves blown off
E very day it gets windy
R ocks start to blow.

Jakihya Boyce (7)
Longmoor Primary School, Long Eaton

Summer

S ometimes people have barbecues

U sually you go to the seaside

M ostly people see flowers on the way

M um sees lots of squirrels come out

E veryone sees leaves grow in summer

R un everywhere around you.

Jack Cook (6)
Longmoor Primary School, Long Eaton

My Name

A pples are tasty

B ats fly in the night

I ce cream is tasty

G oosebumps are scary

A nts are itchy

I gloos are cold

L ollies are cold.

Abigail Cranfield (5)
Mapplewells Primary School, Sutton in Ashfield

My Name

A nt
A pple tree
L ollipop
E ager
I gloo
G rass
H air
A bigail.

Aaleigha Brown (5)
Mapplewells Primary School, Sutton in Ashfield

Thunder

T hunder is as noisy as an elephant snoring
H orrifying, terrifying and blazing
U p in the sky I can hear the thunder roaring like an angry tiger
N othing but lots of thunder
D arkness comes from the dark, dark sky
E arth is full of lots of thunder
R eal thunder crashing in the sky.

Yazlin Sheikh (7)
Mornington Primary School, Nuthall

Sunshine

S unshine is hot and warm
U p in the blue, wonderful sky
N ice and warm sun shining on me
S un is as warm as the playground
H appy children playing in the sun
I love the sun shining on me
N ow the sun has gone in I am sad
E nd of the day I go to bed.

Freya Bird (7)
Mornington Primary School, Nuthall

My First Acrostic - Poems From The East Midlands

Snow

S now is twirling from the sky
N o one is inside
O utside they are throwing and falling in the white snow
W e can make a white snowman as tall as a mountain.

Jacob Morning (7)
Mornington Primary School, Nuthall

Snow And Wind

Snow

S now is twirling from the blue sky
N ow people are having fun in the snow
O w, there's the cold, freezing snowman
W ow, what a nice, cold, snowy day.

Wind

W ow, lots of swirling leaves blowing
I am having a really good time in the leaves
N ow the leaves are swirling from the blue sky
D ancing, twirling from the blue sky.

Hana Ahmed
Mornington Primary School, Nuthall

My First Acrostic - Poems From The East Midlands

Snow

S now is freezing and fantastic to play with
N ever comes in the summer
O ften snow shuts down schools
W e like playing in the snow.

Lauren Thorpe (6)
Mornington Primary School, Nuthall

Wind And Snow

W hite, strong, blowing through your hair
I nvisible, blowing in the air
N orth wind, south wind, which way wind
D ragging in the air.

S melling great hot chocolate
N oisy children shouting
O ver freezing outside, nice and warm inside
W hite, deep snow on the ground.

Natasha Khosla (7)
Mornington Primary School, Nuthall

My First Acrostic - Poems From The East Midlands

Snowy, Sun And Rain

S uch a beautiful sight
N ice and fluffy
O ver the mountains of ice
W hite and gleaming
Y ou can make a snowman.

S unlight
U mbrella on top of you
N ow you can play.

R un in the puddles
A nd then you can leap
I n the wet
N ow you can play.

Charlotte Hindson (7)
Mornington Primary School, Nuthall

Sunny And Snowy

S piky flames
U nder shade
N ice weather
N ever cold
Y ou can play in the sun.

S nowflakes twinkle
N ice snowflakes twinkling
O n a snowy day you can catch snowflakes
W hat an amazing snowflake
Y ou can play with snow.

Ethan Wright (7)
Mornington Primary School, Nuthall

My First Acrostic - Poems From The East Midlands

Snowy, Sun And Icy Day

S oft and white
N ow you can play in the snow
O n the ground I can see snow
W hite and fluffy
Y ou can make a snowman

S unlight
U mbrella so it doesn't burn you
N ow you can swim

I ce skating
C old day
Y ou can play outside if your mum or dad say

D angerous when it is icy
A day that I see
Y ou can go ice skating.

Aimee Canavan
Mornington Primary School, Nuthall

Wind

W indy, cold
I n the wind you can fly a kite
N ow it is windy it will get colder
D angerous because it can rip houses.

Charlotte Kirk (7)
Mornington Primary School, Nuthall

My First Acrostic - Poems From The East Midlands

Thunder

T he noise is very loud
H urting lightning
U nder the ground
N aughty lightning
D angerous like rain
E xtremely loud
R aining hard.

Libby Dolman-Milner (6)
Mornington Primary School, Nuthall

Sunny, Ice And Lightning

S piky, hot flames
U nder shadow
N ice, lovely weather
N ever, never cold
Y ou can have an ice lolly

I t is icy
C old fingers
E yes can see ice cubes

L ight and shiny
I can see it in the sky
G reat in the sky
H igh in the air
T umbling down
N ice in the air
I think it is lovely
N ight is lovely when lightning is in it
G reat when I look in the sky.

Nathan Robinson (7)
Mornington Primary School, Nuthall

Sun, Rain And Cold

S corching hot
U nder shade
N ever cold

R unny water
A lso cold
I ncredible wind
N ever hot

C old as ice
O n a cold day you wear thick clothes
L ovely and cold
D efinitely freezing.

James Kirk (7)
Mornington Primary School, Nuthall

Weather

W hirling wind
E xtreme power
A staggering heat
T hrashing thunder
H ot, burning sun power
E xtremely hot sun
R acing rain.

Harry Franklin
Mornington Primary School, Nuthall

My First Acrostic - Poems From The East Midlands

Snowstorm

S now is very cold and it freezes me up
N ow the snow is drying up from the sun's heat
O ther times when snow comes down it makes a little noise
W hen it snows I make a snowman
S nowstorms are very heavy
T he snow is a winter kind of weather
O n the
R oad when it's snowy it's very slippery
M y snow is very cold.

Shiv Vasi (7)
Mornington Primary School, Nuthall

Storm

S torm makes a big bang and sparkles

T iny drops are called rain

O h, some go in the snow

R aindrops

M ini drops pitter-patter.

Joshua Harris-Owen
Mornington Primary School, Nuthall

Sunshine And Snow

S un is light
U mbrella so you don't get burnt on your head
N ight changes into sun
S hiny in the light
H ands are getting warm by the sun
I like the sun
N ow the sun has changed to night
E ver change night to light in the morning

S now is icy
N ow the snow has gone
O n a snowy day I like snow, do you?
W ow, look at the snow!

Ellie Parkes (7)
Mornington Primary School, Nuthall

Windy And Sun

W indy as a machine
I s cold as ice
N o dabbing or blowing people over
D angerous
Y ou can dance in the breeze

S wim in the sea
U n-cross
N obody's cross.

Mya Sandhu-McKenna (6)
Mornington Primary School, Nuthall

Sunshine

S un is hot
U nder the shade
N ever look at the sun
S easide visits are fun
H appy day on the beach
I n the sea we can play
N ever burn all the day
E verybody happy in the sun.

Bradley Francis (6)
Mornington Primary School, Nuthall

Hailstorm

'**H** urry up, a hailstorm has started

A ny longer I will lock you out

I don't want to go out without an umbrella

L ook out, it's getting heavier, that's my umbrella.

S uper quick, get inside before I lock you out!'

'**T** easer, you wouldn't lock me out.'

'**O** h yes I will

R ight, I'm locking you out.'

'**M** um, let me in, let me in.'

Caashim Kotze
Mornington Primary School, Nuthall

My First Acrostic - Poems From The East Midlands

Blizzard

B lizzards are horrid
L ike a tornado in an
I rregular motion
Z oom, goes the blizzard
Z oom it goes
A s it destroys the town
R uins the city
D oom is on the loose.

Ryan Wigg (7)
Mornington Primary School, Nuthall

Snowstorm

S now is beautiful
N ow children are going
O ut more. The
W eather is astounding
S nowflakes flutter and twinkle to the ground
T all snowmen are fun to make
O ut the children go
R un, I hear that a lot of
M ums and dads are having fun.

Nadia Zeidan (6)
Mornington Primary School, Nuthall

Snowstorm

S ome people like to play in the snow and make a snowman
N o one likes to catch a cold
O nly some people don't like to make a snowman
W e like to have snowball fights
S now is fun to play with
T he snow is fun, it's very cold and foggy
O n the snow it is very dangerous
R unning on the ice
M ore pieces of ice.

Sophie Westbury (6)
Mornington Primary School, Nuthall

Raindrops

R ainy days are really fun
A nd sometimes they make watery puddles
I n the rain, when the raindrops fall, it tickles your tiny, tiny nose
N ow the sunshine comes out to make us happy with its yellow face
D rums go banging for joy because it's a very bright day
R aindrops go pitter-patter, pitter-patter and it never stops raining
O h no, hailstones, they're going
P itter-patter, pitter-patter all day long
S unshine, raindrops and hailstorms are all kinds of weather.

Shivani Handa (7)
Mornington Primary School, Nuthall

Rainbow

R ain comes splattering
A nd spitting down quietly
I n the playground
N ow the sun comes out brightly
B eautiful rainbows come arching out on sunny days
O ver my head the rainbow goes
W ait for the sun and rain to come again on sunny days.

Hannah Davies (7)
Mornington Primary School, Nuthall

Rain Spots

R ain hits the ground
A nd you can't stop it
I jump in puddles and it's fun
N o one can

S top me when I'm having fun
P itter-patter, the rain is coming
O h yes, it's fun on
T his rainy day
S top, it's getting warm.

Ishaan Jumbu (7)
Mornington Primary School, Nuthall

My First Acrostic - Poems From The East Midlands

Rainstorm

R ainy days are fun
A nd you can jump
I n lots of puddles, In the wind rain falls down heavily
N ow the rainstorm is fading away we will
see the sunshine and a rainbow
S ee the beautiful sight of the rainbow
T o see the gold on the
O ther side of the rainbow, climb on it
R ainy days come in spring, summer or autumn, and in winter
M ay sunshine follow the rain.

Paridhi Pande (7)
Mornington Primary School, Nuthall

Night

N ice, dark, lovely night

I like the night

G lowing moonlight

H orrible, disturbing night

T he wet rain.

Owen Burrill (7)
Oakham CE Primary School, Oakham

My First Acrostic - Poems From The East Midlands

Hedgehogs

H amster is crawling in the night
E at the hay
D amp in the night
G reep Street
E ek! A bee is coming to me
H ow can I catch my ball?
O n my roof
G et a wasp
S mile at a lamb.

Philippa Stevenson (6)
Oakham CE Primary School, Oakham

Bats

B ats are really bad
A nts are not asleep at any time
T onight I am going to see nocturnal animals
S ee the darkness is light and people are in bed.

Leah Crawford (6)
Oakham CE Primary School, Oakham

My First Acrostic - Poems From The East Midlands

Owls

O ld flashlight bird
W ild meat-eater
L azy day bird
S leepy daylight bird.

Louis Hibbitt (6)
Oakham CE Primary School, Oakham

Bats

B adgers are nocturnal
A s I walk about in the night
T onight is owl night
S ince animals like me, I like them.

Lucie McKie (7)
Oakham CE Primary School, Oakham

My First Acrostic - Poems From The East Midlands

Nocturnal

N ight-time is when nocturnal animals come out
O wls are nocturnal
C ute little bats
T uck in little owls
U nwanted nocturnal animals
R idiculous little bats
N ice baby hamsters
A nnoying little bats
L ittle possums.

Teigan Palmer (7)
Oakham CE Primary School, Oakham

Bats

B aby bats are cool
A ll bats eat moths
T onight I saw a baby bat
S cary bats can fly.

Chloe Hannah (6)
Oakham CE Primary School, Oakham

My First Acrostic - Poems From The East Midlands

Bats

B lack wings make me fly
A sleep in the day I am
T riangle ears I use to hear
S cary creatures, bats!

Angus Diggle (7)
Oakham CE Primary School, Oakham

Bats

B ats hunt at night
A lot of bats
T he bats are lazy
S cary with no eyes.

Joshua Robertson (6)
Oakham CE Primary School, Oakham

My First Acrostic - Poems From The East Midlands

Bats

B ut they hunt
A t night they hunt
T hey can fly
S he can eat.

Igor Lesney
Oakham CE Primary School, Oakham

Bats

B ats are good
A lthough their eyes don't work
T hey can't see very well
S *queak, squeak.*

Alice Aylward
Oakham CE Primary School, Oakham

Night

N asty noises in the night
I like the night
G reat nocturnal animals come out at night
H edgehogs protect themselves with their spikes
T iny bats come out at night.

Jessica Falconer (6)
Oakham CE Primary School, Oakham

Night

N octurnal animals do not sleep in the night

I nteresting animals

G ood animals

H ard to catch their food

T errifying bats.

Jack Cooper (6)
Oakham CE Primary School, Oakham

My First Acrostic - Poems From The East Midlands

Hamster

H airy hamster
A nocturnal animal
M ummy hamster
S illy
T idy
E ating hamster
R olling.

Georgia McNeill (6)
Oakham CE Primary School, Oakham

Toys

T oys are fun
O range cars are zooming
Y ellow monsters are scary
S pider-Man is a superhero, he is red.

Isaac Rudd (4)
St John the Baptist CE Primary School, Spalding

My First Acrostic - Poems From The East Midlands

Garfield

G iant ginger cat
A lways followed by Odie
R oaming around London
F inds himself lost
I n a castle he ends up
E njoying being a big fat cat
L asagne is his favourite food
D ancing makes him one cool dude.

Lewis Haythorn (5)
St John the Baptist CE Primary School, Spalding

Ryan

R eally happy
Y ou can count on me
A nd I am a good boy
N ever naughty.

Ryan Gadd (5)
St John the Baptist CE Primary School, Spalding

My First Acrostic - Poems From The East Midlands

My Daniel Poem

D aring
A ctive
N oisy
I nteresting
E nergetic
L ovely.

Daniel Plant (6)
St John the Baptist CE Primary School, Spalding

Lambs

L ively and leaping
A lways very soft
M aking noises
B aa, baa
S pring must be here.

Toby Keen (5)
St John the Baptist CE Primary School, Spalding

My First Acrostic - Poems From The East Midlands

My School Is The Best

S t John's is nice because it has helpful teachers

C hildren play and use the equipment

H ave to wear a uniform

O pening doors for people is helpful

O n goes the white board

L isten then you will learn.

Caitlin Seymour (5)
St John the Baptist CE Primary School, Spalding

Rainbow

R ain falling on one side
A nd sun shining on the other
I look up . . .
N ow I am surprised . . .
B eautiful colours shining in an arc
O ver the rainbow
W ill there be a pot of gold at the end?

Ellie Blackbourn (6)
St John the Baptist CE Primary School, Spalding

My First Acrostic - Poems From The East Midlands

Superman

S trong and mighty
U p in the air
P eer in the sky
E veryone can see
R acing through the air
M an flies rescuing
A ll people in danger
N ever be scared.

Oliver Keen (7)
St John the Baptist CE Primary School, Spalding

Artists

A rtists are especially good at art
R emembering scenes, patterns and designs
T o make beautiful pictures
I nk, paint, charcoal, brushes, pens, pencils, fingers are
S ome interesting things to use in art
T hey take their pictures to the shops to be
S old to decorate people's houses.

Max Bland (7)
St John the Baptist CE Primary School, Spalding

My First Acrostic - Poems From The East Midlands

My Rabbits

A tiny white spot with a
L ovely twitching nose, some
B rilliant black eyes and a sparkle in her toes
A lba!

S tupendous patch of fluff on grass
H er tummy glows like light through glass
Y ou wouldn't believe how soft she was.

Lia Carter (7)
St John the Baptist CE Primary School, Spalding

Spider-Man

S winging through the air, launching webs from his hands
P eter is now Black Spiderman, his
I dentity changed, he chases the Green Goblin, with such
D anger ahead. His senses are alert and his
E nergy is high. The people in the street below call out to Spidy
R acing away, his enemy is lost in the darkness.

'M ove faster, Spidy, he's getting away,'
A nd with that, Spider-Man launches his web, lassoing the Green Goblin
N ow the danger is gone, the people are safe and Spider-Man is the greatest.

Harvey Wirkowski (5)
St John the Baptist CE Primary School, Spalding

Horses

H obbies for some
O r friends for life
R ide all day long
S ee them play and
E at some grass until the
S un goes down to bed.

Hope Meadows (7)
St John the Baptist CE Primary School, Spalding

Hippopotamus

H appy
I n the water
P addling
P laying with the
O thers
P ounding to his dinner
O n the bank
T ummy full up
A drink of water
M ust be needed
U nder the water
S *plash.*

Caitlin Langford (6)
St John the Baptist CE Primary School, Spalding

Jamie

J ammy
A nnoying
M uddy
I ntelligent
E nergetic.

Jamie Bertolaso (7)
St John the Baptist CE Primary School, Spalding

James Bond

J ames Bond, 007
A lways on a mission
M otoring through the hills
E very day chasing villains
S omeone stole his plane

B rave and mighty
O pening and closing cases
N obody can beat him
D anger is nothing.

Harry Harman (6)
St John the Baptist CE Primary School, Spalding

My First Acrostic - Poems From The East Midlands

Garden

G ardening is good exercise
A nd gardens are lovely to look at
R epeated weeding keeps it clear
D on't forget to water
E lse your plants will die
N ice to play in your garden.

Ellie Whitcombe (7)
St John the Baptist CE Primary School, Spalding

Saint John's

S itting down and working hard
A fter school clubs and
I nteresting lessons
N ice friends to play with and
T eachers helping everyone

J olly children playing games
O nly at playtimes
H ome time is at 3.15pm and
N ow it's time to go
S chool is fun!

Charlie Wensak (7)
St John the Baptist CE Primary School, Spalding

Butterfly

B utterflies are pretty

U p in the sky

T he beautiful rainbow

T he flowers are pretty

E very time, I go out

R ainbows are pretty

F lowers are pretty to smell

L et us go on holiday

Y ou are really pretty.

Ocea-Lily Jarvis (5)
St John the Baptist CE Primary School, Spalding

Bear

Bear walked and the he went home because there was a problem. He kept popping in and out because there kept being a problem

Eventually he called someone

And then he got

Run over and was never seen again.

Erin Neve Freeston (4)
St John the Baptist CE Primary School, Spalding

My First Acrostic - Poems From The East Midlands

Doctors

D octors help you if you break a bone
O ff the X-ray they tell you if you have broken a bone
C all them if you are ill
T ake your tablets and medicine
O peration is painful
R ing for an appointment.

Novaya Bedward (7)
Sneinton CE Primary School, Sneinton

Nurse

N urses help you get better
U tell them where it hurts
R ing for help
S tay safe when they are coming
E veryone jokes about each other.

Jack Nuqul (7)
Sneinton CE Primary School, Sneinton

My First Acrostic - Poems From The East Midlands

Doctor

D octors help you when you feel sick
O peration
C ut your skin open
T ake your medicine
O pen all hours
R ing the doctor for your appointment.

Shakira Daniel (7)
Sneinton CE Primary School, Sneinton

Nurse

N ever let you down
U se bandages
R eady to help you
S aving people's lives
E mergency hospitals.

Amelia Strangwick (7)
Sneinton CE Primary School, Sneinton

My First Acrostic - Poems From The East Midlands

Nurse

N urse works in the night
U nwell people
R escue people
S ave people
E veryone is looked after by the nurse.

T'arnrie Simpson (6)
Sneinton CE Primary School, Sneinton

Army Guard

A rmy run after people
R elive
M oney
Y ou cannot get past

G uard
U se your weapons
A lot of people come to join the army
R un fast
D o not fall over.

Stevie-Lei Kinniburgh (7)
Sneinton CE Primary School, Sneinton

Shahaab

S miles a lot
H ome time
A mazing
H elpful
A dventurous
A lways nice
B ouncy.

Shahaab Ahmed (6)
Sneinton CE Primary School, Sneinton

Chantelle

C lever
H elpful
A lways caring
N ever sad
T aking care
E very day I smile
L oving people
L ike chocolate
E ating pizza.

Chantelle Allwood (6)
Sneinton CE Primary School, Sneinton

My First Acrostic - Poems From The East Midlands

Space

S olar system
P lanets
A stronauts
C raters on the moon
E xploring the stars.

Kate Armitage (6)
Sneinton CE Primary School, Sneinton

Amaan

A ngry
M ad
A lways silly
A lways driving
N aughty.

Amaan Aslam (6)
Sneinton CE Primary School, Sneinton

Space

S tars
P lanets
A stronauts
C omets
E verywhere.

Joshua Colledge (6)
Sneinton CE Primary School, Sneinton

Space

S un is in space

P lanets go around at a slow pace

A liens from different galaxies

C omets are named, like Halley's

E arth is where we live.

Jocelyn Do (6)
Sneinton CE Primary School, Sneinton

Space

S un
P eace
A liens
C old
E xciting.

Joshua Musson-Screen (5)
Sneinton CE Primary School, Sneinton

Fola

F ola helps her mum
O range
L aughs a lot
A good friend.

Fola Okanlawon (5)
Sneinton CE Primary School, Sneinton

My First Acrostic - Poems From The East Midlands

Gareth

G ood
A lways nice
R ead a lot
E ating is my favourite thing
T apping
H am is my favourite food.

Gareth Pearce (5)
Sneinton CE Primary School, Sneinton

Caeden

C an be a dog
A te an egg
E ats pizza
D own I go
E cho
N ice things.

Caeden Perkins (5)
Sneinton CE Primary School, Sneinton

My First Acrostic - Poems From The East Midlands

Emma

E ating
M ore food
M ini Emma
A untie.

Emma Sargent (6)
Sneinton CE Primary School, Sneinton

Snake

S lithery
N asty or nice
A dder
K ills rats
E ats meerkats!

Lauryn Hewitt (5)
Stanhope Primary School, Gedling

My First Acrostic - Poems From The East Midlands

Coral

C heeky am I
O range juice
R unning, I am fast
A lso I can dance
L ipstick is great.

Coral Frost (5)
Stanhope Primary School, Gedling

Summer

S ummer is sunny and bright
U mbrellas shade us from the light
M erry children in the sun
M aking games and having fun
E veryone's playing on the beach
R acing and making sandcastles.

Emily-Jayne Sturt (7)
Stanhope Primary School, Gedling

Fireworks

F ire
I n the sky
R ound
E very November
W hoosh!
O range glowing
R ed stars
K eep me awake
S parkling stars.

Holly Lamont (6)
Stanhope Primary School, Gedling

Cats

C ats are living creatures
A dog is too
T amzin likes to cuddle cats
S o much, they are soft as can be.

Tamzin Forrester (7)
Stanhope Primary School, Gedling

My First Acrostic - Poems From The East Midlands

Spring

S pring is when we start to sow
P lants and seeds begin to grow
R eproduction brings new life
I like honey from the beehive
N esting birds chirp and sing
G lorious, colourful spring.

Benita Rodman (6)
Stanhope Primary School, Gedling

Pebbles

P ebbles is my kitten
E very day I play with her
B ecause I love her very much
B alls are her favourite toys, she cases them
L ots and lots
E arly in the morning she miaows until I get up
S he then purrs and sits with me, she's my best friend.

Amy Mosby (6)
Stanhope Primary School, Gedling

Rain

R ain is dripping
A wet day
I s blue and dark
N ot nice.

Alex Sturt (5)
Stanhope Primary School, Gedling

All About Me

F lynn is never naughty
L ovely and lively
Y elling a lot, sometimes quiet
N ever eats oranges
N ever eats Brussels sprouts.

Flynn Perkins (6)
Stanhope Primary School, Gedling

My First Acrostic - Poems From The East Midlands

Ballet Dancer

B eautiful dancers in the room
A ll holding hands
L ight feet skip perfectly
L ike swans gliding on a lake
E legant and graceful
T urning round and round

D ancing, leaping and standing on my toes
A round the stage, I skip now
N ew dances to learn
C lap, clap, clap, tap, tap, tap to the music
E ach dancer moves to the music
R ehearsing for the performance.

Nia Everitt (7)
Stanhope Primary School, Gedling

Roald Dahl

R oald Dahl is the best
O h how I love his books
A ll of them are funny
L oved by children all over the world
D azzling words in each book

D elightful characters like Willy Wonka
A mazing illustrations
H ow I love the titles
L iterally the best author.

Georgia Wardle (7)
Stanhope Primary School, Gedling

My First Acrostic - Poems From The East Midlands

Dinosaur

D iplodocus went *stomp, stomp, stomp*
I guanadon chewing the plants
N ests filled up with eggs, watch out for
O viraptor stealing the eggs
S keletons in the ground
A ll over the world they are found
U ltrasaurus is one of the biggest of all
R emember the dinosaurs!

Joseph Willey (7)
Stanhope Primary School, Gedling

Spring

S pring is lovely
P urple flowers come out
R abbits come out in the field
I nsects come out to play
N ew leaves grow on the trees
G oats grow bigger.

Kye Wilson (5)
Sycamore Primary School, Nottingham

My First Acrostic - Poems From The East Midlands

Spring

S pring is special
P ick flowers
R abbits hop
I nsects crawl
N ests are made
G row.

Sabian Mehmetaj (5)
Sycamore Primary School, Nottingham

Spring

S pring is beautiful
P ick daffodils
R eally bright sun
I nsects come out to search
N ew green grass
G reat flowers.

Chloe Wilson (6)
Sycamore Primary School, Nottingham

My First Acrostic - Poems From The East Midlands

Spring

S pring is lovely
P ink flowers become big
R abbits hop
I nsects come out
N ew life comes out
G oats turn big.

Dylan Powdrill (6)
Sycamore Primary School, Nottingham

Billy

B illy is good at skipping
I ncredible friend
L ovely son
L ikes apple juice
Y oungest in my family.

Billy McGinty (6)
Sycamore Primary School, Nottingham

My First Acrostic - Poems From The East Midlands

Jacob

J ust love playing on my DS
A pples are my favourite fruit
C limbing trees
O ldest in my family
B illy is my best friend.

Jacob Jansons (6)
Sycamore Primary School, Nottingham

Lashea

L ove being good
A ble to get to school on time
S ometimes I am good
H elpful to my mum
E xcellent at painting
A dding and taking away.

Lashea Francis (7)
Sycamore Primary School, Nottingham

My First Acrostic - Poems From The East Midlands

Mikhia

M ikhia is good at football
I like fish
K ind and friendly
H appy at home
I like playing football matches
A nimal lover.

Mikhia Walters (7)
Sycamore Primary School, Nottingham

Sausage

S izzling in the pan
A tasty snack
U mmm sausages are nice
S mall sausages
A tasty lunch
G reat as a hot dog
E at me with chips and beans.

Christian Healy (7)
Walter Halls Primary School, Mapperley

Burger

B ig and tasty
U nbelieveably delicious
R eally yummy in my tummy
G reat in a bun with melted cheese
E at me because I am scrumptious
R elish is on me.

Imogen Hamlin (6)
Walter Halls Primary School, Mapperley

Strawberry

S crummy, yummy in my tummy
T asty and juicy
R eally red
A nice healthy snack
W onderfully delicious
B ut sour
E verybody loves strawberries
R ipe and sweet
R eally nice with cream
Y ou can eat the seeds.

Aisha Jobe (7)
Walter Halls Primary School, Mapperley

My First Acrostic - Poems From The East Midlands

Strawberry

S weet, juicy, lovely and smooth
T asty with pips inside, but you can eat them
R ed and delicious
A scrumptious, squidgy snack
W ould you please eat me because I'm so yummy
B ig and juicy
E verybody eats me for a healthy snack
R ipe and ready to eat
R eally nice, you would want to eat me every day
Y our tummy will love them.

Tamyra Sawyers (6)
Walter Halls Primary School, Mapperley

Crisps

C runchy and hard
R eally tasty
I come in lots of flavours
S ometimes I come in different shapes
P ut me on your plate.

Caitlin McCullough (7)
Walter Halls Primary School, Mapperley

My First Acrostic - Poems From The East Midlands

Apple

A delicious healthy snack
P eel it and eat it
P op the pieces in your mouth
L ovely, nutritious treat
E nergy snack.

Jasmine Bird (7)
Walter Halls Primary School, Mapperley

Cupcake

C ake is delicious
U nder the top is cream or jam
P eople love cupcakes, they are lovely
C ome and eat me
A tasty treat and scrumptious
K eep me fresh in a tin
E verybody likes cupcakes.

Wendy Ncube (7)
Walter Halls Primary School, Mapperley

Grapes

G rapes are green and purple and delicious
R ound and squidgy
A grape is one of your five a day
P eople love to eat bunches of grapes
E xcellent snack
S it down and eat some.

Maizie Simm-Grant (7)
Walter Halls Primary School, Mapperley

Crisps

C runchy, salty and tasty
R eady salted is my favourite
I t is a scrumptious snack
S picy is one of the different flavours
P eople love munching tasty crisps.

Ashley Edwards (7)
Walter Halls Primary School, Mapperley

Pineapple

P ineapples are lovely and healthy
I nto your mouth
N ice and delicious
E at me because I'm scrumptious
A sweet
P eel me then eat me
P rickly and pointy
L ovely and juicy
E at me because I'm a sweet treat.

Elizabeth Fisher (7)
Walter Halls Primary School, Mapperley

Peas

P eas are good for you
E at me for your dinner
A yummy, tasty vegetable,
S ometimes you squash me with your fork.

Andrew Jamson (6)
Walter Halls Primary School, Mapperley

Cake

C an be eaten at a party
A yummy and delicious treat
K eep me in the tin
E at me if you can.

Amy Cunliffe
Walter Halls Primary School, Mapperley

Beans

B eans are a healthy food
E at me on toast
A yummy snack
N ice with sausage and chips
S aucy, saucy beans.

Ryan Bates (6)
Walter Halls Primary School, Mapperley

My First Acrostic - Poems From The East Midlands

Apple

A delicious, crunchy apple, juicy snack
P ips inside of me
P lenty of juice pours into your mouth
L ovely and sweet
E at me every day.

Poppy Bawden (7)
Walter Halls Primary School, Mapperley

Crisps

C runchy, tasty and hard
R eady salted is my favourite
I am kept in a packet
S picy and yummy
P eople love to eat me
S ometimes I am different flavours.

Shourya Bhandari (6)
Walter Halls Primary School, Mapperley

My First Acrostic - Poems From The East Midlands

Cake

C reamy and delicious treat
A party cake for a birthday
K eep me in a fridge
E at me because I am lovely.

Henry Tien (7)
Walter Halls Primary School, Mapperley

Cake

C reamy, fluffy and tasty
A birthday treat
K eep me in a tin
E at me, I am yummy and delicious.

Selicia Hickling (7)
Walter Halls Primary School, Mapperley

My First Acrostic - Poems From The East Midlands

Crisps

C runchy and spicy
R eally tasty
I t's very salty
S uper, super yummy
P owerful flavours
S o salty, your eyes go watery.

Makaay Ross (7)
Walter Halls Primary School, Mapperley

Crisps

C runchy and hard
R eally tasty
I come in a packet
S ometimes spicy
P lease eat me because I'm yummy
S ometimes I'm in different flavours.

Ethan Newstead (7)
Walter Halls Primary School, Mapperley

My First Acrostic - Poems From The East Midlands

Curry

C olourful, spicy and hot
U nderneath is a pile of rice
R unny like a liquid
R eally tasty for your dinner
Y ummy, scrummy.

Jeneba Kanneh-Mason (6)
Walter Halls Primary School, Mapperley

Crisps

C runchy, scrummy and yummy in my tummy
R andom flavours
I mpressive taste
S crumptious and delicious
P op me in your mouth.

Oliver Thomas-Roche (7)
Walter Halls Primary School, Mapperley

My First Acrostic - Poems From The East Midlands

Horse

H orses gallop
O ver a fence
R iding on a road
S ome horses eat grass
E very horse runs around.

Kaliyah Sanghera (5)
Walter Halls Primary School, Mapperley

Monkey

M onkey swings

O ver a branch

N ext it eats a banana

K icks a coconut

E very monkey sits down

Y ou see them in a jungle.

Rio Foster (5)
Walter Halls Primary School, Mapperley

Bats

B ats flying
A t night
T o the cave
S ee bats outside.

Thomas Justice (6)
Walter Halls Primary School, Mapperley

Giraffe

G iraffes are funny looking
I t is yellow and brown
R eally long necks
A nd live in Africa
F ast runners
F alling over
E ating leaves.

Marian Eleshinnia (6)
Walter Halls Primary School, Mapperley

My First Acrostic - Poems From The East Midlands

Tiger

T igers eat meat
I t roars at me
G rowling and spitting
E ars twitch
R oars for meat.

Mia Harvey (5)
Walter Halls Primary School, Mapperley

Rabbit

R abbit eats carrots
A rabbit hops
B ig tail
B unnies are cute
I t has cute ears
T he bunny lives in a burrow.

Kaira McGregor
Walter Halls Primary School, Mapperley

My First Acrostic - Poems From The East Midlands

Snails

S low-moving
N ear a tree
A ll snails slither
I t has a shell
L ittle snails live in the garden
S nails are safe from a tiger.

Adina Brown (5)
Walter Halls Primary School, Mapperley

Monkey

M ummy cuddles baby monkey

O n a branch in the forest

N ight-night baby monkey

K icking leaves and wood

E asy climbing trees

Y oung monkey rolls on the ground.

Shannon Campbell (6)
Walter Halls Primary School, Mapperley

Lion

L ions roar
I t's growling
O ver a fence
N ight hunting
S its on the floor.

Adrian Chamberlain (6)
Walter Halls Primary School, Mapperley

Spider

- **S** piders in spider school
- **P** eople see spiders
- **I** t spins webs
- **D** igs a hole
- **E** ats flies
- **R** uns around.

Caleb Bird (5)
Walter Halls Primary School, Mapperley

My First Acrostic - Poems From The East Midlands

Butterflies

B utterflies flutter, beautiful,
U p in the sky,
T o the white clouds
T he butterfly is nice
E ach has got beautiful patterns
R eally pretty
F riendly to people
L ikes you
Y esterday I saw a butterfly.

Hayden Barrows-Gayle (5)
Walter Halls Primary School, Mapperley

Nature

N ests have eggs in
A nd
T rees have leaves on
U nderground there are worms
R abbits like hopping around
E veryone likes nature.

Ellis Davenport & Jack Owen (6)
Willow Farm Primary School, Gedling

Flowers

F lowers are beautiful
L ilies grow in the ground
O utside flowers
W onderful flowers
E xtremely amazing
R ain makes flowers grow
S un is flowers' favourite thing.

Carter Pateman & Rosie Walker (6)
Willow Farm Primary School, Gedling

Nature

N ests are in the tree
A pples are red and golden
T rees sway in the wind
U nderground there are snails
R abbits, chicks and lambs
E veryone loves nature.

Mckensie Withers, Lilly Hamed, James Martin, Izabelle Hamblin & Matthew Brookes (6)
Willow Farm Primary School, Gedling

My First Acrostic - Poems From The East Midlands

Myself

M y name begins with W
Y ou can see me playing in the park
S ometimes I play in the sand
E very day I play on my bike, and I
L ike
F ish and chips.

William Barclay
Willow Farm Primary School, Gedling

Myself

M y mum is an architect
Y ou do work and play at my school
S till I am nice
E ating is good for me
L uckily I have a house
F inally in this poem it is the end.

Bob Banks (7)
Willow Farm Primary School, Gedling

My First Acrostic - Poems From The East Midlands

Myself

M y name is Elyse
Y ou can see I like dancing
S inging too
E veryone thinks I'm funny, and I
L ike
F ruit.

Elyse Tizzard (7)
Willow Farm Primary School, Gedling

Myself

M e, I myself like football

Y es - goal!

S ee me now,

E asy, cool dude,

L eon is on my team

F ootball is the best.

Josh Jackson
Willow Farm Primary School, Gedling

My First Acrostic - Poems From The East Midlands

Animals

A nimals are cool
N ot like fruit
I love animals
M y dog is called Suki
A ll animals have a brain
L ots of animals are vicious
S ome animals can see in the dark.

Freddie Talbot (7)
Willow Farm Primary School, Gedling

Myself

M y name is Laila
Y ou will see me playing with the Plasticine
S ometimes you will see me in the water
E very day my dad picks me up from school and I
L ike
F ish and chips!

Laila Ahmed (7)
Willow Farm Primary School, Gedling

My First Acrostic - Poems From The East Midlands

My Family

M y mum is number one
Y es they're nice

F ish and chips we all like
A mazingly wonderful
M y dad is number one
I love my family
L ots of lovely people are in my family
Y ou can see it!

Holly Wild
Willow Farm Primary School, Gedling

Myself

M y name begins with A
Y ou can see me playing with the underwater toys
S o are you going to the park?
E very special day I get
L ovely
F ish and chips.

Ava Hemsley (7)
Willow Farm Primary School, Gedling

My First Acrostic - Poems From The East Midlands

Pokémon

Pikachu is rubbish

Onix is cool

Kadabra is alright

Empoleon is wicked

Monferno is fantastic

Oh! I

Never stop playing with my Pokémon.

Frazer Deabill
Willow Farm Primary School, Gedling

Myself

Myself is clumsy
Yuck - seafood!
Sometimes I am hyper
Even I can be tired
Like, I really like playing
Fish and chips are gorgeous.

Taryn Pike (6)
Willow Farm Primary School, Gedling

My First Acrostic - Poems From The East Midlands

My Cat

M y cat begins with S
Y ucky cat!

C at power!
A clean cat now she's used her
T ongue.

Xander Beck (7)
Willow Farm Primary School, Gedling

My Friend

My best friend is Sophie
You will see me playing with her on the field

Friends forever
Really funny and very kind
I like her a lot
Every day I play with Sophie
Nearly all day
Dancing on Wednesdays.

Caity Cooke (7)
Willow Farm Primary School, Gedling

My First Acrostic - Poems From The East Midlands

My Friend

My friend is George
You can see him outside playing

Friday - we both have an ice cream
Roar! he always goes
It always hurts my ears
Especially when he does it loud
Nobody is fun like George
Diving all the time.

Michael Shepherd
Willow Farm Primary School, Gedling

My Dog

My dog barks when the doorbell goes
Yes, it's annoying

Doggy power
Oh no, Nelly hurt herself
Go, Nelly go!

Scarlett Leigh
Willow Farm Primary School, Gedling

Pig

P iglet
I nteresting
G ood.

Sonny Chapman (4)
Willow Farm Primary School, Gedling

Fish

F ast
I tch
S wim
H appy.

Millieann Willis & Benjamin Shaw (5)
Willow Farm Primary School, Gedling

Bird

B lackbird

I nteresting

R aven

D uckling.

Murray Wild, Charlton Rooke, William Redfern, Lucy Middleton & Billy Jones
Willow Farm Primary School, Gedling

Dog

 usty

 utrageous

G rowl.

Oliver Holmes, Casey Griffiths, William Galloway & Alyssa Everington-Dale
Willow Farm Primary School, Gedling

My First Acrostic - Poems From The East Midlands

Cats

C ute
A mber
T ail.

Eve Blissett, Leon Blakey, Florence Banks, Hannah Bacon & Niamh Bailey (5)
Willow Farm Primary School, Gedling

Flowers

F lowers grow from the ground

L ovely colours

O range petals

W et weather feeds flowers

E very plant needs sun

R oses

S mell nice.

Grabrielle Fowler & Max Humber (6)
Willow Farm Primary School, Gedling

Nature

N ature is all around
A nd
T rees are green
U p high in the blue sky
R ain helps plants grow
E veryone loves it outside.

Zoe Hyland-Freshney (6)
Willow Farm Primary School, Gedling

Plants

P lants grow

L ovely leaves

A nd

N ice flowers

T all plants

S un and water help plants grow.

Connor Macvickas & Joseph Warren (6)
Willow Farm Primary School, Gedling

Nature

N ests are in trees
A nimals are nice
T he leaves fall off trees
U nder the ground there are different animals
R ainbows are colourful
E ggs are in nests.

Maiya Needley & Drew Chapman (6)
Willow Farm Primary School, Gedling

Earth

E verything lives on Earth
A nts carry leaves
R ed flowers
T rees grow high
H ot sun shines.

Harvey Widdowson & Malachi Gregg (6)
Willow Farm Primary School, Gedling

My First Acrostic - Poems From The East Midlands

Animals

A nts are tiny
N ests are where birds live
I nsects creep and crawl
M onkeys swing in trees
A nd nocturnal animals
L ike night
S limy snakes.

Harry Bates & Emily Gomersall (6)
Willow Farm Primary School, Gedling

Nature

N ests are for birds
A nimals are born
T omatoes are red
U p in the trees are birds
R ainbows are different colours
E xtremely wonderful.

Millie Godward & Ben Morris (6)
Willow Farm Primary School, Gedling

My First Acrostic - Poems From The East Midlands

Flowers

F lowers are pretty
L ilies grow on the ground
O ld flowers die
W ater makes
E very flower grow
R ain makes flowers grow
S unshine makes flowers grow.

Tom Oldershaw & Casey Lydon (6)
Willow Farm Primary School, Gedling

Young Writers Information

We hope you have enjoyed reading this book - and that you will continue to enjoy it in the coming years.

If you like reading and writing poetry drop us a line, or give us a call, and we'll send you a free information pack.

Alternatively if you would like to order further copies of this book or any of our other titles, then please give us a call or log onto our website at www.youngwriters.co.uk.

Young Writers Information
Remus House
Coltsfoot Drive
Peterborough
PE2 9JX
(01733) 890066